Life of the Snail

Life of the
SNAIL

by Theres Buholzer

A Carolrhoda Nature Watch Book

 Carolrhoda Books, Inc./Minneapolis

*Thanks to Dr. Donald Gilbertson of
The James Ford Bell Museum of Natural History,
Minneapolis, Minnesota, for his assistance
with this book*

This edition first published 1987 by Carolrhoda Books, Inc.
Original edition published 1984 by Kinderbuchverlag KBV Luzern AG,
Lucerne, Switzerland, under the title SCHNECKENLEBEN
Copyright © 1984 Kinderbuchverlag KBV Luzern AG
Translation from the German © 1985 by J.M. Dent & Sons Ltd.
Adapted by Carolrhoda Books, Inc.

Manufactured in the United States of America

LIBRARY OF CONGRESS CATALOGING-IN-PUBLICATION DATA

Buholzer, Theres.
  Life of the snail.

  Translation of: Schneckenleben.
  "A Carolrhoda nature watch book."
  Includes index.
  Summary: Describes the physical characteristics,
habits, and natural environment of the snail.
  1. Snails—Juvenile literature. [1. Snails]
I. Title.
QL430.4.B8513   1987   594'.38   86-21544
ISBN 0-87614-246-3 (lib. bdg.)

  2 3 4 5 6 7 8 9 10 97 96 95 94 93 92 91 90 89 88

From spring until early fall, large numbers of land snails can be seen in gardens and in wooded areas. Their beautiful shells and their silver trails attract attention to this small, slow creature. Land snails have different bodies and habits than water snails, and, although land snails are common, most of us know surprisingly little about them.

Since I wanted to know more about the occupants of those spiraled shells, I decided to see if I could keep snails satisfactorily in captivity. On my balcony, I prepared a small enclosure made to resemble snails' natural surroundings and filled it with half a dozen snails.

Snails need plenty of moisture and shade. I sprayed them frequently, using rain water whenever I could, and covered the enclosure with a piece of cardboard. Because they were living in an enclosure, I was able to observe and photograph them, by night as well as by day.

This book follows a year in the life of the captive snails. Snails living in the open spaces of the outdoors may have different patterns of behavior.

Snails belong to a large group of animals known as **mollusks**. Mollusks are animals that have soft, unsegmented bodies with no inner skeletons. I filled my enclosure with three different **species**, or kinds, of snails including the grove snail, the copse snail, and the helix garden snail. All of these species thrive in moist, shady environments, and they are easily found in gardens and wooded areas.

The grove snail, also called the banded snail (scientific name *Cepaea nemoralis*), is pictured in the top right photograph.

Normally it has five dark bands varying in thickness. These bands follow the shape of the **whorls**, or turns, of the shell, but the number can vary, and sometimes the bands of color are run together or are absent. The shell's background color also varies considerably. Usually it is a clear yellow but can range from white to brown as well as pink or rose-red.

The copse snail, also called the tree snail (scientific name *Arianta arbustorum*), has a brown shell with yellow markings and a black stripe (center photograph). Unlike the grove snail, its body is black.

The helix garden snail (scientific name *Helix pomatia*), is shown in the bottom photograph. Often called the edible snail, this species is listed as *escargot* on the menus of many restaurants. Also known as the vine snail, Roman snail, apple snail, and burgundy snail, the helix garden snail is the largest of the three species in my enclosure. Its shell ranges in color from cream or gray to pale yellowish brown and has up to five whorls and a similar number of narrow dark bands that follow the spiral shape of the whorls. Its body can extend to an overall length of up to 4 inches (10 cm).

The most noticeable part of a snail is its shell. Without its shell, a snail would dry up and die. It can withdraw into its shell as protection against enemies, cold, and heat. A snail's shell is partially made of **calcium carbonate** and is quite hard. It is covered with a natural glaze, which eventually wears off as the snail gets older.

Around the rim of the shell opening is a hard, outward-turned lip, which can be seen clearly in the top right-hand photograph. The shell is marked by a series of **growth rings**, or grooves, which look like tiny furrows. As the shell grows, it produces these rings. The growth of a snail's shell is an amazing process. Just inside the lip of the shell opening is a collar known as the **mantle**. The mantle is made up of living cells that take chemicals from the food, water, and other materials the snail eats and change them into shell material. This shell material is added on to the existing shell material, creating growth rings and increasing the size of a snail's shell so that it coils to display more and more whorls. The shell goes on growing until the snail is about three years old.

The part of the snail's body that is pushed out of the shell is called the **foot**. At the front of the foot is the head with its two pairs of **tentacles** (one short pair and one long pair).

The snail's tentacles move in many directions—forward, backward, up, and down. The upper, longer pair carries the snail's eyes, the black spots on the tips of the tentacles. These eyes do not help the snail see objects very well. They probably are only able to distinguish light and dark as well as give the snail a shadowy picture of objects.

The shorter tentacles are very sensitive to touch, and they help a snail to "see" by feeling objects within their reach. They also help the snail to "hear" by detecting vibrations. Both sets of tentacles can be pulled back inside the snail's head, seeming to turn inside out as they collapse from their centers until they disappear into the snail's head.

Snails move by rippling the muscles in the **sole**, or bottom, of the foot. Their progress is slow, usually covering less than 3 inches (7.6 cm) in a minute. They move slowly because their shells are large and heavy in proportion to their bodies. By letting out a stream of mucus from a gland at the front of the foot, snails form a layer of protective slime between the ground and their bodies. This creates a track which they use to slide smoothly and easily over uneven surfaces.

In the photographs on the right, you can see a snail emerging from its shell. First comes the tail end of the foot, then the front end of the foot with the head, and lastly the rest of the foot between the two ends. Snails often retreat into their shells for protection. If you touch a snail's tentacles, the snail will pull into its shell head first with the rest of the foot following. After its body is drawn in, the snail's mantle expands to fill any space in the shell opening.

Two other outer parts of a snail's body, its **pneumostome**, or respiratory pore, and its mouth are small and less visible, but both are very important. When a snail is on its back, body withdrawn into its shell, the mantle is clearly visible. On the edge of the mantle is the pneumostome, an opening which leads into a cavity beneath the shell. The cavity contains the snail's **lung**, a thin sack of blood vessels that enables the snail to get oxygen from the air to use in its body. In the photograph to the right you can clearly see the whitish mantle and the pneumostome, which opens and closes as the snail breathes.

The small mouth hole is on the underside of a snail's head, below the tooth-shaped upper lip, which you can see in the photograph to the left. The snail's method of feeding is unusual. Inside the mouth is the **radula**, a rasplike tongue covered with thousands of sharply pointed teeth that are arranged in rows. The radula can be pushed out and moved back and forth to scrape off small pieces of food for the snail to draw back into its mouth.

The helix garden snail, grove snail, and copse snail are all found in shady, moist places. They avoid the sun and so move and feed mostly at night, although warm, rainy weather may cause them to become active by day.

Many different kinds of animals prey on snails, among them birds, frogs, toads, insects, and small mammals such as rats, skunks, and raccoons. Broken pieces of shell littering a small area are a sign that a bird has recently made a meal of a snail. Some birds get the snail meat by pulling the snail out of its shell, but other birds will hold the snail in its beak and beat it against a stone to shatter the shell, leaving pieces of shell scattered on the ground.

Man is another of the snail's enemies. Sprays that are deadly to snails are used in many gardens to keep snails from eating plant leaves. The helix garden snail has even more to fear from humans, for many people consider this snail delicious to eat. Indeed, the demand for these edible snails is so great that in places they have been **exterminated**. Several European countries now take special measures to protect them. Because there are fewer and fewer of these snails, some people are raising them in captivity for commercial purposes.

Sometimes, if a person steps on a snail's shell, or if an object falls on it, the shell will get cracked or crushed. If the shell is crushed and air reaches the snail's body, the snail cannot survive. A surface crack that allows no air to get to the body is minor damage, and the crack in the shell will mend in time. After accidently damaging the shell of one of the snails in my enclosure, I covered the deep crack with plaster to keep the shell airtight. The plaster gradually became built into its shell, making this snail very easy to identify.

Snails are most active during the seasons with the greatest amount of moisture. They pair off, lay eggs, and spend a great deal of time eating. The snails in my enclosure also spend time riding on each other's shells, although this may not be common behavior in more open surroundings.

In warm, dry weather, snails become inactive. This inactivity during the summer is called **estivation.** At this time, snails look for a wall or tree trunk where, after attaching themselves with slime, they withdraw into their shells. They prefer to attach themselves to smooth surfaces, like the pane of glass shown in this photograph, or they burrow into a sheltered place, lying with their shell openings facing up. They seal the entrance to their shells with a thin film of mucus, which dries in the air. The mucus seals of snail shells each have a tiny hole in them to allow air to get into the shells so that the snails can breathe.

Snails can estivate for days or weeks. While it is estivating, the snail does not eat, and its body functions slow down. Moisture usually brings a snail out of estivation. In captivity this can be done by sprinkling water directly on the seal of the shell.

Snails' food consists mainly of broad-leaved plants, juicy green food, and vegetables, but they also eat decomposing vegetation and sometimes soil. An important part of a snail's diet is calcium, one of the elements used in producing its shell. Snails get calcium from stones, cement walls, and soil. I give my snails a mixture of crushed limestone and flour to give them the calcium they need.

The snails in my enclosure frequently return to a regular roosting place where they are often found in clusters after searching for food. They touch one another with their tentacles or the soles of their feet, or simply move about investigating their surroundings. Small snails often ride on the backs of larger snails. Even snails of the same size occasionally go for rides. The rider eventually falls off, leaving its mount's shell smeared with slime or earth. The snails then clean their shells with their mouths as the grove snail is doing in the bottom right photograph. It is probable that snails in their natural surroundings do not gather together the way that snails in an enclosure with limited space do.

Early summer is mating season for snails, the time when they begin to search for their mates. Helix garden snails have an unusual courtship ritual. They touch each other with their tentacles, bringing their bodies together and pressing their soles against each other. Body against body, they rear up to their full height, rubbing their heads together and swaying from side to side. This play may continue for hours. Before mating begins, each of the two snails in turn thrusts a **love-dart** into its partner's sole. The love-dart is a tiny, chalky spike, about 1/5 of an inch (5 mm) long, that is formed in a special pouch. These jabs with the love-dart stimulate mating and encourage the whitish **reproductive pore** to stick out from the right-hand side of each snail's head.

Most land snails are **hermaphrodites**, which means that each snail produces both **sperm**, or male reproductive cells, and **eggs**, or female reproductive cells. Although each snail has both male and female reproductive cells, they cannot make their own eggs **fertile**. They must find a mate with whom they can exchange sperm in order to produce fertilized eggs. One snail deposits a **spermatophore**, or packet of sperm, into its partner's reproductive pore. The receiving snail then transfers its spermatophore to the first snail in the same way. In each snail the sperm and eggs unite to produce fertilized eggs. Each snail now will be able to lay fertilized eggs when it is time. All three of the species described in this book will normally be three years old before they are fully mature—or before they are capable of pairing off and breeding.

After mating, the partners of each species remain together for some time before separating. Helix garden snails sometimes even sleep clamped together.

Depending on the species of snail, the eggs are ready to be laid about one month to two months after mating. A snail that is about to lay its eggs selects a quiet spot with loose, moist soil in which to make a nest. Using its muscular foot, it digs a hole in the ground. Carefully squeezing 30 to 60 eggs out of the reproductive pore, it deposits them in the hole before covering the nest with soil and leaving. The process of egg laying can take an entire day. The eggs are small, tough skinned, and are a dull, whitish color. Eggs of the grove and copse snails are about 2/25 of an inch (2 mm) long, while the helix garden snail's are 1/5 of an inch (5 mm) long.

Incubation, or the time needed for the embryos to develop inside the newly laid eggs, takes about two weeks. The newborn snails are hatched with their shells already formed. Upon hatching, they eat the remains of their eggs before feeding on the chalky soil around them. It can take as long as three weeks for them to work their way slowly to the surface. Only then do they start eating green food.

To start with, the shell of a newborn snail is transparent, soft, and delicate. A newborn's shell is the same size as the egg from which it is hatched. The body, though, is slightly longer when fully outstretched.

Since the shells are still transparent, it is possible to see how the tiny snails withdraw into them. The shells look like glass balls. At this stage they have only two whorls; fully grown snails have four or five whorls.

Different types of snails develop in different ways. The helix garden snail grows comparatively quickly, its shell color soon fading to gray-brown. The copse snail's shell is reddish brown and its body is dark from the beginning.

The greatest changes occur in the development of the grove snail, which is pictured here at two different stages. Its shell grows slowly and remains transparent for a long time. Either in the winter or the spring following the summer of its hatching, the grove snail's shell changes from being almost colorless into colors of rose-pink, pure yellow, or bands of black.

During the fall, snails spend most of their time eating in preparation for winter. In the winter, snails **hibernate**, living on the reserves of fat in their own bodies. Hibernation is a longer period of inactivity than estivation so snails need to store more fat and be more prepared. To get ready for hibernation, snails look for a secure, warm place where they can bury themselves under leaf litter or in a hole that they dig into the soil.

After sealing the opening to the shell with a thick protective layer of slime, snails go into an inactive state of deep rest. The winter's 'sleep' lasts at least three or four months. To encourage my own snails to hibernate, and as a protection against cold, I place heaps of beech leaves in their enclosure. Beech leaves do not decompose, so their shelter makes an ideal winter hiding place for hibernating snails.

During hibernation, a snail breathes very slowly, and the little air it requires comes through a tiny opening in the seal of its shell.

Helix garden snails prepare for the winter by encasing their shell openings in a hard layer of chalk about 1/25 of an inch (1 mm) thick. This protects them from both cold and dryness. The colder the weather the more deeply the snail withdraws into its shell and the greater the number of protective layers of chalk it manufactures—up to as many as six separate layers.

Throughout the winter, a snail's only source of nourishment is the reserve of fat that is left in its body from the overeating of the fall. By the time spring comes, it has lost a lot of its body weight. As the weather grows warmer and the soil is softened by rain, the snails wake up from their long rest and emerge from their hiding places.

Each snail uses its foot to break through the covering that seals the opening of its shell. It then digs its way through the soil up to the surface and at once sets about searching for fresh green food. When the helix garden snail emerges in the spring, its chalky seal is pushed out in one piece and left lying on the ground like the chalk seal pictured above.

Upon emerging in the spring, the snails gorge themselves until they are full almost to bursting. It is essential for them to put on weight in order to build up the strength they have lost through the long winter. Not all snails survive the winter. Some may not have stored enough fat in their bodies, the winter may have been unusually severe, or the spot in which they chose to hibernate proved unsuitable. The empty shell of a snail that did not survive the winter is here being used as a shelter by a smaller snail.

Snails that survive the winter explore their surroundings, leaving behind them a series of glistening slime tracks.

The length of a land snail's life varies. One grove snail and one copse snail lived in my enclosure for five years. Since they laid eggs during their first year in captivity, they could not have been less than three years old on arrival.

They must, therefore, have lived at least eight years. Land snails living in their natural surroundings probably do not live this long. Being regularly sprinkled, fed, and cared for, my snails lead an agreeable life and have given me many interesting and satisfying hours of observation and study.

GLOSSARY

calcium carbonate: a substance that is a combination of two minerals. Calcium carbonate is found in nature in bones and shells.

egg: a female reproductive cell

estivation: when an animal is in a temporary state of inactivity during the summer

exterminate: to get rid of completely, usually by killing off

fertilize: to unite a sperm and an egg so that an embryo may develop

foot: the part of a snail's body that sticks out of the shell

growth rings: grooves on a snail's shell created by the addition of new shell material

hermaphrodite: an animal or plant having both male and female reproductive organs

hibernate: to pass the winter in an inactive state. During hibernation, all body functions slow down.

incubation: the period of time necessary for an embryo inside a newly laid egg to develop into an animal

love-dart: a tiny, chalky spike used by some snails to stimulate mating

lung: the respiratory organ of air-breathing animals

mantle: a tissue of living cells that lines the shell opening of shell-bearing mollusks and produces shell material

mollusk: a member of a large group of animals, each having a soft, unsegmented body with no inner skeleton

pneumostome: an opening that allows air to flow into the cavity that contains a snail's lung

radula: a tongue present in many mollusks that is covered with tiny, sharply pointed teeth and is used to scrape off small pieces of food

reproductive pore: a whitish organ that sticks out from the side of a land snail's head during mating

sole: the bottom of a snail's foot. The muscular rippling of the sole moves the snail along.

species: a group of animals or plants that share similar characteristics

sperm: male reproductive cells

spermatophore: a packet of sperm

tentacle: long, fingerlike knobs extending from the heads of many animals. A snail's tentacles carry its eyes and other sense organs.

whorl: one of the spiral turns in a snail's shell

INDEX

ABOUT THE AUTHOR

Author-photographer **Theres Buholzer** is a social worker who works with children. She became interested in snails when children at a daycare center where she was director began collecting snails to study them. Since then she has made these small animals her hobby, observing how her captive snails live in their enclosure on the balcony of her home in Zurich, Switzerland. *Life of the Snail* is her first book for children.